IN
WINDSOR FOREST

A Cantata for Mixed Voices

MUSIC ADAPTED FROM THE OPERA
SIR JOHN IN LOVE

R. VAUGHAN WILLIAMS

VOCAL SCORE

MUSIC DEPARTMENT

OXFORD
UNIVERSITY PRESS

NOTE

Orchestral Score and Parts may be hired

An arrangement of this Cantata, for S.S.A.,
is also published.

IN WINDSOR FOREST

No. I
THE CONSPIRACY
('Sigh no more, ladies')
(For women's voices)

Words by
SHAKESPEARE

Music adapted from the Opera
'SIR JOHN IN LOVE'
by R. VAUGHAN WILLIAMS

* May be sung by a solo voice if preferred.
Orchestral Score and Parts may be hired.

*Tutti from here

4

5

fraud of man was ev - er so since Sum - mer first ___ was

First was lea - vy, ___ Then sigh not so

First was lea - vy, ___ Then sigh not so

lea - vy Then sigh not so But let them

but let them go, ___ Con - vert - ing all your

but let them go, ___ Con - vert - ing all your

go and be you blithe and bonny Con - vert - ing all your

7

No. 2
DRINKING SONG
('Back and side go bare')
(For men's voices)

Words by
JOHN STILL

Music adapted from the Opera
'SIR JOHN IN LOVE'
by R. VAUGHAN WILLIAMS

Allegro pesante (2 beats in the bar)

Back and side go bare, go__ bare, Both foot and hand go__ cold; But,

bel - ly, God send thee good ale e - nough, Whe - ther it be new__ or__

13

No. 3
FALSTAFF AND THE FAIRIES
(Round about in a fair ring-a)

Words by
SHAKESPEARE
RAVENSCROFT and LYLY

Music adapted from the Opera
'SIR JOHN IN LOVE'
by R. VAUGHAN WILLIAMS

A-bout him, fairies, sing a scorn - ful rhyme; and, as you sing,

pinch him to your time. —

Pinch him pinch him black and blue,

Sau - cy mor - tals must not view What the Queen of stars is do - ing, Nor pry in - to our fai - ry wooing

29

Pinch him and burn him and pinch him and burn him and turn him, till candles and starlight and moonshine be

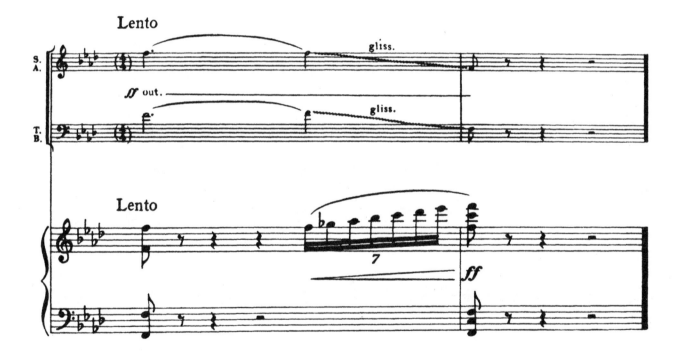

Lento

Lento

No. 4
WEDDING CHORUS
(See the Chariot at hand)

Words by
BEN JONSON

Music adapted from the Opera
'SIR JOHN IN LOVE'
by R. VAUGHAN WILLIAMS

34

swords, through seas whi-ther she would ride _____

swords, _____ through seas whi-ther she would ride _____

swords, through seas whi-ther she would ride _____

swords, through seas whi-ther she would ride _____

f cantabile

dim.

Do but look on her

43

No. 5
EPILOGUE
(Whether men do laugh or weep)

Words from
Campion and Rossetter's Book of Airs

Music adapted from the Opera
'SIR JOHN IN LOVE'
by R. VAUGHAN WILLIAMS

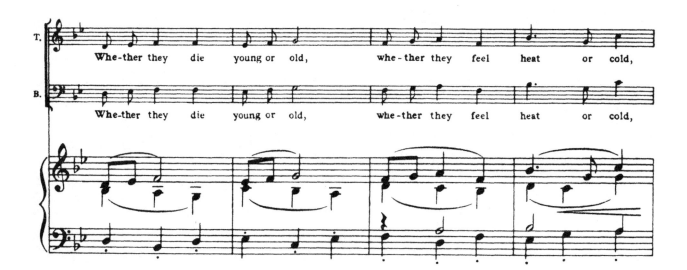

T. Whe-ther men do laugh or weep, whe-ther they do wake or sleep,

B. Whe-ther men do laugh or weep, whe-ther they do wake or sleep,

T. Whe-ther they die young or old, whe-ther they feel heat or cold,

B. Whe-ther they die young or old, whe-ther they feel heat or cold,

48

50

Halstan & Co. Ltd., Amersham, Bucks.

OXFORD UNIVERSITY PRESS